Hanan Issa is a mixed-r̲   ̲ned at numerous events a̲   ̲een featured on both ITV W̲   ̲has been published in Ban̲   ̲ɔon mag, Lumin, sister-hood magazine and MuslimGirl.com. Her winning monologue was performed at Bush Theatre's Hijabi Monologues. She is the co-founder of Cardiff's first BAME open mic series 'Where I'm Coming From'. She is also one of the 2018 Hay Writers at Work.

My Body Can House Two Hearts

Hanan Issa

Burning Eye

Copyright © 2019 Hanan Issa

The author asserts the moral right under the Copyright, Designs and Patents Act 1988 to be identified as the author of this work.

All rights reserved. No part of this publication may be reproduced, stored in a retrieval system, or transmitted, in any form or by any means without the prior written consent of the author, nor be otherwise circulated in any form of binding or cover other than that in which it is published and without a similar condition being imposed on the subsequent purchaser.

This edition published by Burning Eye Books 2019

www.burningeye.co.uk

@burningeyebooks

Burning Eye Books
15 West Hill, Portishead, BS20 6LG

ISBN 978-1-911570-75-2

To Mama, for giving me dragon poems.
To my *rih al mursala* for, well, it all.

Allah, the most Merciful, taught me that there has never been a man capable of containing two hearts in his body. I view the many interpretations of this in more than a literal sense. Audre Lorde taught me that women have an immense capacity for interdependence and compassion and that these are essential tools in dismantling patriarchy. My heritage is woven from two places overflowing with culture, language and history. I would like to think I have enough love inside me for all of it.

Contents

Lands of Mine	9
Jean	10
Ten Men	11
Adab	12
Croesawgar	13
Converts	16
Better Version of Bravery	17
Si'luwa's Song	18
Lugha	19
I Don't See Colour	20
Offa's Coin	23
My Body Can House Two Hearts	25
Fairouz and French Toast	26
The Human Pig	27
Austrian Hands	28
Qawwam	29
Arabic Dancing at a Wedding	30
Beauty and Blood	31
Paradise of Poets	32
Watching him eat strawberries	33
Glossary	34

Lands of Mine

Hen wlad fy nhadau occupies my thoughts.
Blazing rage and bullets piercing dreams of Baghdad.

Al Askari is gone. I roll up paper, twist out the middle,
then crumple it to resemble the damaged Malwiya –

even the spot where a lovesick girl jumped to join the deaths
of Mongol hordes and wise men lying forgotten in the dust.

Baba, you promised we would eat at the rotating restaurant.
But someone like my son, nothing like my son, finds comfort

in thinking he was following orders. As houses collapse,
palm trees extend heavenwards, afraid to look at the painful

detritus below that lights a blinding hiraeth inside me
for *hen wlad fy mamau* – the home I have loved halfly.

I think of my great-grandfather, who breathed in coal dust as he
breathed out kindness; mishtaqeen, gentle George.

From the dark wooden drawers of my nan's Welsh dresser
emerge stories of loyal dogs and fickle flower princesses.

Kan yawma kan, I am a woman of neither here nor there.
Although it is here I have bled and brought forth my child

of more than two places. I gift him with the names
of extraordinary princes, and the stories of my people:

of Fallujah, of Aberfan, of Baghdad, of Caerdydd.

Jean

'You are Welsh first!' my nan always says,
though she can't speak a word of it.
Kids in her school got a rap on the knuckles
for every 'll' caught whispered in the playground.

Growing up, it was Rosie stories at bedtime,
sinking into her softly warmed marshmallow divan.
We woke to grateful chirps outside the window
since Nan always left out bread for the birds.

She liked bringing us breakfast in bed.
Doorstop toast, butter sliced thick like cheese,
cut into not-quite-triangle shapes
'cause she nibbled the burnt edges first.

Cheeky kids – we still mimic her Valleys voice,
tricking her into saying the shahadah
or asking her to call my dad a kalb.
She swears she has no idea what it means.

Nan prayed with us once. In a room full of women
wrapped in susurrant cotton and prayers.
She stood next to me, head bowed,
enamoured of the quiet loyalty of another tongue.

Ten Men

We say *timman* for rice, not *ruz* like other Arabs.
I heard a rumour that the word came from the British.
When Iraqi farmers refused to feed the colonisers,
shipments of Ten Men rice arrived from India.
Heaved onto the backs of men, stubborn as hakaka,
with sweat on their faces and revolution in their hearts.

'You are next,' the bags of rice teased. Like the Ten Men,
my great-grandmother came to Iraq on a boat.
An Indian bride for a soldier whose eyes turned further east.
Although my great-grandmother's skin mimicked belonging,
the faces around her used letters she couldn't pronounce;
she ate bitter noomi basra, craving the fiery comfort of home.

She gifted her daughter with Indian features
and the knowledge of biryani that burns your tongue.
My family were taught to turn their eyes westwards,
settling on my mother – a lighter bride for the bloodline.
They try to bury the story of a woman who sang Hindi songs.
Triumphant, they nickname my palest sister 'Snow White'.

Adab

The rug matches the vase on the shelf.
Women fit thickly like trees in a forest.
'Make sure your socks are matching.'

Invasive floral perfume, pendulating
earrings clock the minutes you have to stay.
'Just say, *Alhamdulilah,* you are fine.'

Your chai-pouring skills, into delicate
gold-rimmed glass, are observed with mock
indifference. 'Always take a biscuit.'

Looking over the rim of their cups,
they appraise the servility in your teeth,
the forgiveness in your hips.

Croesawgar

> *In 1966 Jeff Edwards was the last survivor to be pulled from the rubble of the Aberfan mining disaster in Wales. He was eight years old.*
> *In 2016 Omran Daqneesh was pulled from rubble in Aleppo, Syria, after surviving a Russian airstrike. He was five years old.*

His face is covered in dust
as they pull him out of the rubble.
Confused, he looks for the familiar reality
that existed moments before he was buried alive.
He searches for his friends –
so impatient to start the holidays –
but his childhood died that day.

Fifty years later, another boy emerged,
face full of blood, dust and sorrow.
His blank stare engulfed the world:
the voyeurs of suffering
in a painful echo of the past.
But the past is a foreign country,
as LP Hartley says.
With foreign food, and foreign ways,
a foreign language,
as different as Aleppo to Aberfan.

A woman from Syria said,
'Wales reminds me of home.'
This place full of fields, farms
and beaches commands you
to belong. Daffodils and rugby,
choirs and coal have caricatured us
into an image as convenient as Lake Australia.
But what about the niqabi woman
speaking Welsh on the bus?

The *ch* of both a Welsh
and Arabic tongue has faced rejection here
and every time someone forgets
the name *Llyn Bochlwyd*,
a piece of the *Mabinogi* disappears.

Last year, 325 refugees were settled in Wales.
Carmarthenshire welcomed fifty-one.
Swansea thirty-three.
Merthyr Tydfil zero.
The Town of Steel made the names
Dowlais and *Cyfarthfa*
known across the world.
Its industry smelted the imagination
of innovators like Isambard Kingdom Brunel.
'The place where modern Wales began.'

But the air turned toxic in the Town of Steel:
pathogens and overpopulation.
'Jobs! Jobs! Where are the jobs?'
Steel men with idle hands.
They hung their heads,
faces dirtied by white not black dust,
trying to forget how useful they could be.
Shedding the coal and the iron
like a refugee loses their cloak of belonging.

Now, turning inwards,
they blame difference for their downfall
and vote to Leave, to close, to reject.
Blinded by misfortune,
proud to remain unaware
that those seeking refuge
have suffered for their own sunken black gold.
It too promises and poisons their veins
as much as Midas' trove.
Can't they see that both are fossil fuels
buried and baked beneath the earth
for greedy hands to grasp and
entomb their unwilling dead?

What difference is there between the suffering
of Jeff Edwards and Omran Daqneesh?
Pulled from rubble,
smothered in dust and blood.
'Wales reminds me of home,' she said.
The dream of belonging sits beneath our soil.

The strength that clings to Welsh language
will not fail by reaching past daffodils and rugby,
proudly pointing to a map, declaring,
'This is the land of *croesawgar*.'

Converts

Standing together in rows,
they are the gentle trees
in whispering fabric
gifted from a friend.
Shoulder to shoulder,
these willows may have wept
for a lost parent or a man
eager to change her name,
but in this forest their roots
spread. Forgive me, they rustle
together, right hand over left
over a heart that has searched
for space in a pew and perfumed
cushion, at the bottom of a glass,
in another's arms. But here
they settle. Here they breathe.
Standing in rows,
turning their trust upwards,
seeing signs

        in
           falling

                    leaves,

dancing bees,
            the rain.

Better Version of Bravery

When the police asked me to describe the girl in the taxi/ I said she was a crying Lynette lying in a self-made bed/ *Help me*, she mouthed through plump pretty lips at the window/ The taxi driver stayed facing forward/ stayed blind as the boyfriend held her against the glass/ I don't blame him for looking away/ The world is unfair and fares are not enough/ His money goes back home like magic/ Slippery paper/ counting the days he stays waking up earlier than he wants to/ *Help me*, she said/ But do I look helpful?/ Most days the fabric eclipsing my mind/ churns a tale as shielded as Shahrazad/ she who stories to prolong her relevance/ but her voice jars/ against the restless chant: the world is nice to white girls, the world is nice to white girls, the world is nice to white girls/ surging into that taxi and as the girl in the back drowns/ all I can hear is the crushing of Christine Blasey Ford's war cry/ *Help me*, she said/ I'll say I called 999 and tried my best/ I'll confess I wish for power like Judge Rosemarie/ In fearless words she sentenced a monster 175 times over/ But it's easy to pick the right side of history in hindsight/ 'Course I would sit next to Rosa/ freedom riding through the consequences/ *Help me*, she said/ her fear and my shame clouding the glass between us/ I looked away as his hands tightened on her neck/ But no one wants to wear the face of a coward on a T-shirt/ so I'll borrow a better version of bravery/ I'll say I did something.

Si'luwa's Song

Hnak ma hnak! I sang:
'Watch this slim waist, this silky hair dance.
See how my breasts know their place.'
Men always sought my song,
always eager to follow the music
of swaying hips and a throaty laugh.
'Come to Hufaidh,' I sang; 'bring me your strong arms
and violent dreams and we will lie below the blooming stars.'

Then I withered.
Then he left.

And these breasts hang over my back.
The grass steams where my stooping shadow touches.
But next to ripe hips and bouncy tits
the power of Enheduanna means fuck-all.

So I found my valuable.
I became my tailored mirror.

And I remembered how to turn garlic into gold,
how to fill a man's eyes.
Now I lick my lover's legs.
My milky bitter tongue stops him running.
Afterwards I toss him back into the river.
Hnak ma hnak! I sing:
'Look at every aged she belied with false compare.'

Lugha

An assured composition,
the confident guttural gh,
haloed,
the nur of Allah's language

eviscerates fruitless scratchings,
plaiting words of Welsh or French,
inept,
tangents lost in shamed prayer.

Like a wounded bird,
its upward basking curtailed,
flailing,
I implore with my patchwork tongue.

I Don't See Colour

I tore off a white stripe
so my trainers looked Adidas.
I begged Mum for the Nike knockoffs
in Bessemer so I could meet
the mean girls' eyes in the playground.
She took that extra shift at the chippy
and her uni work was stained with grease and oil.
I won the 'dole scum' bursary,
an imposter sat in classrooms
next to girls with a timeshare.
But that's not the story you've come to hear.
So I'll start again:

the lines of this box
were scored when I was seven,
and it was a violent drawing.
Trenches cut deeply into my skin.
My skin. My brown turned yellow –
tanned-but-not-so-tanned –
where are you from – pa-la-ta-ble skin.
Light enough for compliment,
dark enough for insult.
'Keep your filthy black hands off my son,' she said to me.
Filthy. Black. Hands.
'I thought I was white like you, Mum?'

Her answer stuck in her throat,
a lump in my chest.
Soon finding the space in between
was the goal, and so I discovered Said,
beginning a louder courtship with Arabic:
'History is written by those who win
and those who dominate.'
But there were too many voices
clamouring left and right.
BAME, MVEMJSUNP,
my status classified and orbit charted,

while Nan implored with songs
and stories anchoring me here.
And it hurt. Walking with heavy feet
from space to space, minding the gaps,
crossing the yellow line, afraid to fall,
three paces ahead in protest of my voice as 'awrah,
of my scarf as a beacon of unbelonging.
Exhausted, I began carving a seat for myself
in Fitzgerald's fields of universal longings
and taught myself to breathe
facing whatever wind

the Anemoi or Mikail send my way.
So watch me spear the next John Chau
who dares to plant a flag on my shore.
Fuck your astonishment at my eloquence,
or your hunger for hijabi victim porn,
O thou foul thief –
I reject your letting, your permission,
I won't be exhibited for the masses
to stare at or save.

But, for all my chanting, here I am,
still inside the box, with nothing to offer
but a traumatic colour.
'I don't see colour,' you say?
Humans are all the same, all equal,
just wilting together in a vase.
But even in black and white,
I'm still a person 'of colour':

at seven my hands were too 'black',
my Adidas stripes weren't white enough.
Mum's hand-stitched hijab
in the uniform colours didn't stop
the teacher's insults.
The yearbook was red when Amy said
I was 'most likely to be a terrorist'
and I wore pink. Purposely, I wore pink

to the event where they pronounced
my name wrong twice.

Of course you don't see colour.
How could you in a world so full of white?

Offa's Coin

> *In 2018, eight-year-old Saga found a 1,500-year-old sword in Lake Vidostern, Sweden.*

Of course, it was Saga who found the sword.
Girl goddess of seeing and poetry.
I cried when I heard how an oracle girl
had unearthed a piece of history to puzzle us.
And oh, how the sword saga binds our stories.

Sweden has buried many Muslims
the world remembers as Viking.
Relearning Allah-embroidered shrouds
that adorn with definition in every careful stitch.
They embraced the ancient and the old divine

seeking eternal life across continents,
death-dreaming of both Jannah and Valhalla.
Is it harder to imagine dark-faced Vikings
or golden-haired warriors sujooding
to the God of sand and Bedouins?

Cardiff rebuilt the Peel Street stones
after the war sandcastled that Tiger Bay taqwa.
Abdul Hamid's restoration is remembered
though you may pray there not knowing his name:
salam, to you, leaving kindness as your legacy.

Middle Eastern ballast bolsters Ebenezer's walls.
Just down there past the job centre, look!
Long may you live, stubborn rocks from possibly Palestine.
And a church built by no churchman: 'the fairest abbey'
has the skilful 'saracen' Lalys to thank.

Lord Henry Stanley rebuilt the walls of Llanbadrig
out of holy love. When he traded cross for crescent,
he blended protection in the blue stained glass.
So don't forget that his shahada testified change
in his heart for the heavens, not the soil underfoot.

And it was Offa's coin that buried '*la ilaha ill Allah*'
in Welsh soil. Some days I choke on that coin:
stamped with a sign somewhat foreign, somewhat forged.
We speak the stories that fit best. So I think
I'll write Saga's sword belonged to a Muslim.

My Body Can House Two Hearts

We say *qalbayn* for 'two hearts'.
Pumping parts through crimson sea.
Tied to lands history split,
I've tried to fit uneasily.

A blazing of blood combined.
Obsess, rewind, frustrate me,
say between two stools I fall,
those boundary walls formed early.

But my body is enough,
gently tough, stretched agony.
Growing a love embracing,
rejecting patriarchy,

no need to shame my peers
or let my fears rat-race me.
Two hearts my body can hold,
so I mould my legacy:

to make space enough for all,
standing tall, I rise, breathe free.
Two hearts – a strength none can take;
love's a lake and the world is thirsty.

Fairouz and French Toast

You always write my name in barbecue sauce on the plate
and now I can't hear a Fairouz song without seeing
your beautiful back flipping egg-soaked bread, pouring
my coffee. She's singing about Beirut: *She tastes like fire and smoke.*
I chew the warm soggy bread, the salty toast and sweet sauce.
You hum along: *You are mine, you are mine.*

The coffee tastes strong, a bit ashy. I picture the fire
and smoke of all the places where they love Fairouz.
'Another piece?' You take my plate and replenish my name.
The coffee leaves debris on my tongue. I want to hold it all –
the breakfast, the music, your back. Even the coffee.
Please, don't stop humming: *You are mine, you are mine.*

The Human Pig

Entry cost tuppence. His friends paid the fee,
clanging it into a tin can. A cluster of Cogan boys crept
past the abandoned Rover, to the back of his parents' pub.
Stood beneath the bedroom window looking up.
Tuppence the boys paid, but Grampy tells us for free.

And we feel like we are there, one of the boys,
stood beneath the bedroom window looking up
at the sickly boy swollen with lead poisoning.
His body, hindered by striped pyjamas, suffocates
at the seams. Buttons cling against the unnatural bloat.

The boys cannot see their friend in this monster's face:
gouged slits for eyes, lips contorted, his maggot fingers reach
for them, imploring. This story, hyperbolised in every telling,
brands us; we laugh and swallow the urge to run away
like the boys back to the safety of our mothers.

Austrian Hands

I watched her hands crochet a tiny daisy
and crack an apple in half like an egg.
She shared stories of an Austrian childhood,
making English taste like a foreigner on the tongue.
Every Eid she spent hours perfecting crispy truffles.
Her powerful hands crafted cornflakes and coconut
into sugary sandcastles that collapsed in your mouth.
I asked her once, foolishly, about what Hitler did.
'No,' she insisted, 'Austrian hands did not make this.'

Qawwam

Our consent is a silence discarded
beneath layers of laws piled like dirty laundry.

'Please, sister, stand on this pedestal just below me.'
'But, brother, paradise lies at my mother's feet, not yours.'

You always held the hijab too tight, a noose leashed
to your stories that begin: *In the Name of Allah*.

Lowering our gaze from the stars, you favour those who repeat,
In the Name of Allah, I love to look at the ground.

But you forget God says our bodies can house two hearts:
In the Name of Allah, our love is much fiercer.

Arabic Dancing at a Wedding

It can be awkward at first: hesitant
tottering heels start forming a circle.
To relieved cheers and the *zaghrouta*,
confident dancers flow into the centre,
swaying, arms up, to Nancy's beat.
We don't dance like the white girls.
No Orientalist bellies ripple;
here, it's all about that butt
and the bigger, the better.
Tying scarves around our hips,
laughing, sweaty, shaking our tits.
On the edges sit older women,
preferring to watch and remember.
Our waists curl hypnotic like smoke.
Twisting hands of flamenco, ballet, bhangra.
Breathing this carefree moment, so vulnerable.
It is here our sexy holds the gaze unburdened.

Beauty and Blood

The Hammar is a marshland area in Nasiriyah, Iraq. Saddam drained the marshes in order to control the Marsh Arabs.
Capel Celyn is an area in North Wales that was flooded in 1965 to provide a greater water supply to Liverpool...

Imagine they drained the Hammar
to flood Capel Celyn: an exchange of tears,
displacing people like chessboard pawns.
Part the whispering reeds' soft curls
and watch smatterings of life drift lost.
As the little Welsh town fills with water,
hear the pained goodbyes of women
who tattoo each other's stories in secret.
History is always the beauty and blood.

Paradise of Poets

Kisses drift to Iraq, dandelion seeds I spread for you.
Seeds, for I want love blooming everywhere they tore you.

I say, 'One day,' feeling the lie in my feet, soaked in dreams,
so jealous of the gifted bottles of sand when I crave more you.

But this land here is sung as the paradise of poets.
So I swallow enough mother tongue to safely store you.

Borders mean nothing to birds murmurating in the sky,
a different dance of survival, a remembering for you.

Buried under dusty bodies weeping oil, Iraq, you remember
burning books for warmth – oh, how they love to war you!

I sit in Wales and think how our hands will never touch, Iraq.
So in every rivulet, every crease of myself, I pour you

and make up dreams of our meeting, Hanan flying
over the *Dijlah*. I wake tasting your winds and roar you.

Watching him eat strawberries

kills me. That familiar ache
in the left side of my chest,
conjured by that smile,
the twin of his dad's delicious face.

He has no idea. I can't breathe because of the sweetness:
the sunlight,
the strawberries,
his face.

It isn't spectacular.
We are sat in the kitchen
with the washing machine
for mood music.

There's a line of dirt under his fingernails. Today, he is
an explorer,
a gardener,
a pirate –

turned forager, scouring
the kitchen for snacks.
He settles on the strawberries
just as I knew he would:

a poetic fruit. I don't know if the moment would be as perfect
with a banana,
an orange,
or grapes.

But I want to stay here,
with his dirt-filled fingernails,
juice trickling down that little chin.
Wallahi, I want to stay here.

Glossary

Lands of Mine

Hen wlad fy nhadau: translates as 'the land of my fathers' and is the title of Wales's national anthem. Most will remember singing it in Welsh lessons or from watching a rugby match. It's ironic that Wales is the land of my mother, not my father, hence my use of the reverse term: *hen wlad fy mamau*.

Al Askari and *Malwiya*: are both mosques damaged by ISIS during their occupation of parts of Iraq. I painted a watercolour picture of the Malwiya minaret and imagined walking up the spiral pathway, but it doesn't look like that will ever happen.

Baba: In secondary school all my friends would call my dad 'Baba', thinking it was his name.

Hiraeth: *ah, hiraeth*. Along with cwtch it will go down in history as one of those words we managed to peddle across the border. Some people say it means homesickness, others say it means longing. According to my Welsh-speaking poet friend Grug Muse, who I trust in all things, it simply means to miss something.

Mishtaqeen: 'I miss you'. My mum and nan speak so fondly of my maternal grandfather George that it sometimes feels like I met, loved, and lost him when they did.

Kan yawma kan: roughly translates as 'once upon a time', but I prefer Zeina Hashem Beck's interpretation: 'there was, and how much there was'.

Jean

Shahadah: that thing you need to say before you die. If you aren't already familiar, you may remember this word from RE lessons in high school. It means to testify. I testify to my belief in Allah. I testify to my love for my nan, who is not Muslim despite being tricked into saying this many times during our childhood.

Kalb: as far as insults go, calling someone a dog in English is fairly mild. Amp that up to calling someone a piece of shit and you get the context of using the word in Arabic. It sounds even better in my nan's Valleys accent.

Ten Men

Hakaka: really onomatopoeic word for the crusty layer of rice at the bottom of the pot. It is a delicacy in Iraqi culture and given to your favourite guest.

Noomi basra: dried limes. Bitter on their own but so tasty in Iraqi soups and stews.

Adab

Adab: manners are really important to Arabs. It sounds obvious since most people appreciate politeness, but there are particular manners to follow when visiting an Arab household. Things like always eating what is offered, which is tough if you don't like it, or always taking things with your right hand, which is tough if you happen to be left-handed.

Alhamdulilah: thank God.

Croesawgar

Croesawgar: welcoming. Croeso is one of the few Welsh words my Arab dad knows the meaning of, and that says a lot, I think.

Llyn Bochlwyd: so the story goes that an old grey stag escaped capture by swimming into the lake. Apparently it has been renamed Lake Australia on tourist maps for non-Welsh speakers' convenience. The erasure of language means the erasure of memory means the erasure of us.

Better Version of Bravery

Lynette: in 1988 Lynette White was murdered and three black and mixed-race men from the Cardiff Docks area were wrongfully imprisoned for her murder. It wasn't until 2002 that the real culprit, Jeffrey Gafoor, a white man, was charged and incarcerated. I'd recommend the BBC Sounds podcast series Shreds for further insight into what is known as 'the UK's worst miscarriage of justice'.

Shahrazad: a character from One Thousand and One Nights. In a nutshell, she had to keep telling stories to save her own life.

Christine Blasey Ford: I remember crying out of frustration and shame following her highly publicised testimony against Brett Kavanaugh. Her courage in speaking out and the subsequent hate she received is an example I think about a lot.

Judge Rosemarie: is the perfect example of female interdependence and empowerment. She has used her privilege and position of power to provide justice for the survivors of Larry Nassar. She allowed over 150 'sister survivors' to give testimony during the court case. She is a queen. Look at her.

Si'luwa's Song

Si'luwa: is a mythical figure from Iraqi folklore with all the best bits of a river witch/selkie/mermaid/siren.

Hnak ma hnak: literally 'here not here'. A traditional form of opening for Iraqi storytelling.

Hufaidh: Iraq's answer to El Dorado. A magical floating island that glows in the dark and is overflowing with ripe pomegranates and buffalo… what's not to like?

Enheduanna: she was the earliest recorded poet in history and lived in Mesopotamia (modern-day Iraq).

Lugha

Lugha: the word means 'language'. I have a complicated relationship with Arabic. It is the language of the Quran as well as so many perfect words. It's also the language I associate with an unsupportive dad and corrupt Muslims. I taught myself how to read Arabic and part of me regrets not being fluent but part of me doesn't really care.

Nur: light. The light that guides you literally and spiritually. The light you see in people's faces when you connect. The light we all so desperately want to find within ourselves.

Offa's Coin

Sujooding: sujood is considered the closest position you can spiritually get to God.

Peel Street: was the first purpose-built mosque in Wales. It was bombed during World War II, restored in 1947, then demolished in 1997.

La ilaha ill Allah: if you aren't already Muslim and you say this, you'll become a Muslim and then it's bye bye bacon for you.

My Body Can House Two Hearts

My Body Can House Two Hearts: I've fallen in love with cynghanedd, as much as I can with my non-Welsh 'patchwork tongue', and this is, in large part, due to Grug introducing me to Mererid Hopwood's wonderful breakdown of the ancient poetic form in *Singing in Chains. Cynghanedd* is designed to be read aloud, so please indulge me by reading this piece out to yourself or anyone who will listen.

Qawwam

Qawwam: refers to the daily responsibility of Muslim men. Over time, reminding a man of his duties, as required by Islamic law, has been replaced by emphasis on his rights. True qawwam, however, is a beautiful, albeit rare, show of strength, love and loyalty that is hard not to admire.

Arabic Dancing at a Wedding

Zaghrouta: when done well the sound makes a statement of happiness and celebration; when done badly it sounds like a frightened turkey.

Paradise of Poets

Dijlah: the Tigris river.

Watching him eat strawberries

Wallahi: Arabs love a good oath, and the highest oath you can make is swearing by Allah's name. Commonly used to demonstrate a point: 'Wallahi I didn't eat your Snickers.'

Acknowledgements

Alhamdulilah.

Thank you, Mama, for standing with your back straight. Grateful for your guidance, love, and sacrifice.

To Aleah, Riyadh, Laith, Kookie and Usayd – thank you for always being supportive when needed and for the harsh bants when needed.

To Nan and Gramps, thank you for being such beacons of love.

To Abdurrashid, hayati, for believing in me, and Yousuf, habibi, for being my sunshine.

To Ameira, Durre, Aisha and Grug – thank you for reading awful drafts, listening to my rants, giving advice, bringing me chocolate or unicorn things, and being just generally fabulous strong women I am humbled to know.

To Ange, Vicky, Sinead, Robyina, Omera, Amanda, Sadia, Taylor, Radha, Rabab, Rachel (H, A, and J), Um, Nida, Fred, Mariyah, Ffion, Asma, Yousra, Hafsah, Sakinah, Lisa, Amanda and Della – thank you for your friendship and sisterly support.

To Abdul-Azim for your article on Muslim history in Wales.

To Shagufta, Bridget, Clive and Adrian for all your encouragement and input.

To all the poets who have helped and encouraged and inspired me. To Audre Lorde and Toni Morrison for being my shaman women. To everyone who comes to Where I'm Coming From and puts up with my voice on that mic. Thank you Zeina for your kindness.

Lightning Source UK Ltd.
Milton Keynes UK
UKHW011325100822
407118UK00004B/1125